Decode Your Mind

Author
Rajesh Sachdev

BLUEROSE PUBLISHERS
India | U.K.

Copyright © Rajesh Sachdev 2024

All rights reserved by author. No part of this publication may be reproduced, stored in a retrieval system or transmitted in any form or by any means, electronic, mechanical, photocopying, recording or otherwise, without the prior permission of the author. Although every precaution has been taken to verify the accuracy of the information contained herein, the publisher assumes no responsibility for any errors or omissions. No liability is assumed for damages that may result from the use of information contained within.

BlueRose Publishers takes no responsibility for any damages, losses, or liabilities that may arise from the use or misuse of the information, products, or services provided in this publication.

For permissions requests or inquiries regarding this publication, please contact:

BLUEROSE PUBLISHERS
www.BlueRoseONE.com
info@bluerosepublishers.com
+91 8882 898 898
+4407342408967

ISBN: 978-93-6452-628-9

First Edition: June 2024

I dedicate this book to all my readers who have the grit to re-wire their leading abilities and create the best version of themselves. Your willingness to bring changes within you inspires me. I feel honoured to share my experiences, and principles, with each one of you. I also dedicate this book to all those who coded my mind by teaching me, making me learn and more importantly inspiring me to deliver my experiences & learning back to society!

My heartfelt gratitude...

Contents

No.	Chapter Name	Page No.
	Preface.	1
	Glossary.	4
01.	Is our brain programmed by Society?	6
02.	Understand your daily life programs.	12
03.	Decode/Read the minds.	25
04.	What more to Decode (DYM & Psychology)	31
	Recap and what's more	36
05.	Emotional Intelligence	39
06.	DYM- A tool to increase your emotional quotient	47
07.	Decode the Situation.	52
08.	Decode the Intention/Feeling.	63
09.	EQ & IQ relationship	72
10.	DYM – Base to the Programming skills.	79
11.	DYM – Base to the Project Management skills	83

Preface

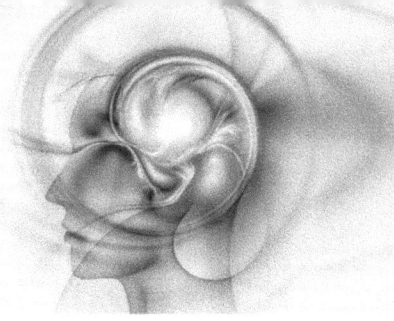

We come across many different kinds of people throughout our lives. Some people appear to be mind-readers, who seem to have the ability to get inside your grey matter while others don't. And we begin to feel that this first set of people probably possesses superpowers, are intuitively high or are they, absolute psychics?

Or are there merely some simple calculations at work?

This book (Decode your mind) and its sequel, book#2 (Code your mind) is my sincere effort to equip you with all these must-have skills.

So read along!

The general thought people have is that we are dissimilar, not only in our attire, dialogue, personality, etc, but we behave or react in our own unique fashion as well. This book will give you a deeper insight into the fact that our dissimilarities are indeed very similar.

LET THE TRANSFORMATION BEGIN!

Millions of codes, every day, are at a tireless run on the silicon chips in your smartphones, watches, laptops,

Preface

printers, television sets, play stations, cars, planes, trains, and almost all electronics fathomable. Today there are far more silicon chips than there are people on this planet.

If you think deeper, you will realize that the human brain works very similar to these silicon chips.

Are we any similar to a computer?
Is our brain programmed?
OR
Is it something far beyond?

Life is an ongoing process and every step of the way we learn. We tend to put in efforts with all our might to become the best versions of ourselves. At various stages of our lives, we get 'loaded' with information by varied means. Whatever has been fed, whether it is society, family, work, we transmit accordingly! All of that becomes a part of our rational and conscious, and many a time subconscious mind too. It has been my observation that the steps that we consciously take in life, be it any given scenario, our reaction signifies the functioning as if a computer is at work. To understand this better please read the first chapter.

Chapters 2 & 3 are an effort to make my readers understand the literal concept of DECODE YOUR MIND that will equip everyone with the steps that are needed to break down/drill down the many attributes of a given situation. The drill-down that I feel is exceptionally

Preface

important, will assist you in navigating the thought process of the other person, and his/her reaction, at that point in time.

Once you advance with this book, you will be able to understand the importance of the emotional aspect of our individuality. Better known as EQ (Emotional Quotient), and how impactful can it be, for the overall growth of self, and cognizance of the people around us. The concepts mentioned in this book will aid towards consistent progress as each and every step of the way you will get the sense of being nurtured to become a finer version of yourself.

The concepts that will be discussed during the course of DECODE YOUR MIND, will give you a deep understanding of the psychology of an individual that will make you a better leader. Furthermore, a discreet insight into Computer Programming and Project Management will also be witnessed, with relevance to decoding the mind.

Glossary

Before proceeding further, I would like to usher into the minds of my readers few terms that we will be frequently using in this book. None of us is untouched from the computer programming and these words. While many of you would be aware of it, others may find it to be relatively new.

So, let us understand these terms from the perspective of the book:

Decode your mind (DYM): A concept that revolves around the fact that the human mind and computer are similar in a way that both follow instructions. Humans build the instructions themselves with their experience, while the computer processes whatever has been fed to it by the developer. Human beings have emotions and other traits that create a particular pattern. On the other side, a computer is a dumb machine because everything is just data for it.

Programming: to understand this word as a layman, we first have to agree that a computer is a dumb machine and it can't do anything on its own. In order for the computer to perform any task / solve any problem, someone (which we call **Developer**) has to feed the step-by-step instructions to tell computers how to solve the problem. This feeding step-by-step instruction to the computer, is **'programming'**.

Glossary

Coding: Developer needs to write in language what computer understand. Feeding these step-by-step instructions using programming language (language which computer can understand), we call it as **Coding.** and the statements we write, are **codes.**

Algorithm: It is a procedure or set of instructions for solving any problem in a finite number of steps that frequently involves repetition of an operation.

Flowchart: It is just a graphical representation of the **Algorithm.** When a developer has to write a program to solve a problem statement, he/she first needs to breakdown the proposed task into smaller steps, and then put it in the pattern of a flowchart/algorithm that is understandable to the peers.

Decode: just like how we have engineering and reverse engineering, similarly, there is coding and decoding. The ability to understand the working of a Code that has been written, is termed as, Decoding.

Now I believe you can relate the concept of DECODE YOUR MIND! If not, just keep reading…

Drilldown: Drilldown is to break down any given task into subparts, or sub-sub parts. It is like zooming 100% of a task and getting a clear picture of the various smaller tasks attached to it. Drilldown helps to find the flow of steps you follow to complete any activity and hence it becomes the base of writing any flowchart / code.

CHAPTER - 1

Is our brain programmed by Society?

*What we are is the outcome of
what we have learnt from society*

When a child is born, he/she knows very little about their environment. They express their feeling by simple signs understood by their mothers. The mother is their first feeder, literally and otherwise. She is the epitome of the highest form of affection, and without her gentle care, none of us would be able to attain our individuality.

Let me now shift your focus from motherly affection to how our first feeder i.e. mother is helping to program a child's brain.

A child cries when he is hungry. This message is in turn interpreted by the mother or caretaker and an appropriate response is shown by the mother which satisfies the need of the child in that situation. In this case, the mother feeds him.

This is a sweet little act performed by the mother, who loves her child unconditionally, where she manages to know the need of the child so well.

Main thing to note in the above example is how a child's mind enters into the coding zone. The above experience develops a code in the brain of the child, which he follows

Is our brain programmed by Society?

in the future. Yes, it's just that simple. If we take a deeper look into this, then we will find that any future expression from the child will be the outcome of the responses that he has experienced earlier and that has been fed into his limited system.

And this is a process that continues throughout our lives, only the feeders keep changing. Sometimes it is the society, family, friends, teachers so on and so forth. As mentioned earlier, we all react in our own way to any action. It also happens that at times our reaction is based on another individual's perception of a similar situation/happening. This could be due to immense faith in that particular person, or our ability to identify with what that person went through. In other words, this is a kind of flowchart that keeps developing/processing at its own pace every day

We are social animals, and meeting people is part of our growing up process. Relatives may stay close or far from us, but we surely do not meet very often. When we meet a relative say, after a prolonged gap, we tend to express our affinity with slight variations in our behavioural pattern. Let us, for instance, explore our varied reactions to meeting different sets of people.

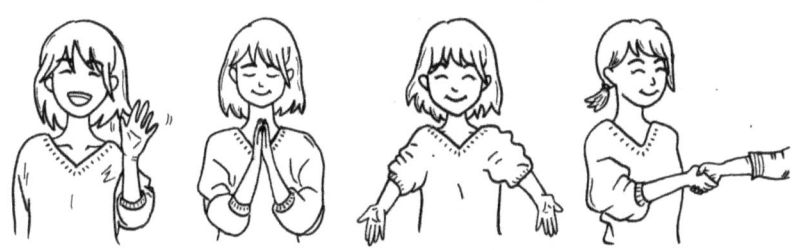

Is our brain programmed by Society?

1. A distant elderly relative -. A maternal uncle comes visiting us once a year so our normal way would be touching their feet, a formal exchange of how everyone was doing in the family, so on and so forth. In India, it is customary that we touch the feet of elders as a token of respect towards them.

Now, this is the flowchart that has been rendered to us since we were very small. We have seen our elders doing it with their elders so we follow in those footsteps. And this has become so grilled in our system that the moment we see an elderly person we bend and touch their feet. The custom has been drilled into our roots. Unlike in other countries, people find it very uncanny when such an act is seen. I remember an incident that I would like to share here. My cousin, who was younger than me, had married to a Britisher, came to India with her husband. My son who was only 4 at the time, bent and touched both their feet. To this the English man literally jumped, and exclaimed, 'what are you looking for, my dear!' this was all too bewildering for my little boy, but the rest of us did have a hard time controlling our laughter! Now the difference of customs is what anybody would observe here, and without a doubt, it is so, but the conflicting attitudes, or 'flowcharts' as I prefer to term them, have been totally opposite in nature that my son ever got, and what the English man ever knew.

2. A middle-aged person - Our normal response to meeting a middle-aged friend/relative/neighbour would

Is our brain programmed by Society?

be Namaste, where we fold our hands as a token of regard. Though this culture has been found in various other lands, so it will not be all that difficult to identify with. As mentioned in the previous example, customary practices emerge without any effort. Just like how touching the feet of the elderly, this folding of hands(namaste)has been inculcated into us for a very long time. So, our acquired format while meeting a middle-aged person would generate the mentioned gesture. We will not have to put in extra effort because we have been told time and again that this is the only way to express polite admiration, and respect.

3. Similar age group - if we were to meet someone of the same age group as ours, our code of conduct toward them would be very different. Right from the way, we look at each other, to the choice of words, and behaviour would have variations as compared to what we talked about in the earlier examples. Here, since there is no age gap, we naturally loosen up a bit, and our process of greeting them is more relaxed. It may just be a hug, a kiss, or 'hello', or a pat on the back along with,' how have you been!' The flowchart that gets activated in this situation, has primarily been the outcome of whatever has been injected into us. And if by chance we were to meet a very close friend after a gap of some months, etc, we would show our anger by saying,' so you finally got time' (time mil gaya), but in reality, we are only expressing sheer love by using these set of words. Our furor to our bosom buddy is actually the outcome of the deep bond that we may

Is our brain programmed by Society?

share. Many burst out crying after they see a loved one after a long gap, while others show their temper. All of these expressions are again the outpouring of the ingredients that have been the main components of our flowcharts. The mental mechanism at work gets aligned to the emotional structure of what has been given to us by society.

4. Small children - When we meet small children, our mind responds in a totally unique manner. We tend to pull their cheeks, or maybe give them a tight hug. The expression of love that we feel for them will come out more in actions than words. Again, it is the sequence of ideas that we have perceived for a long, that activates our action pattern.

My main intention of stating the above-mentioned example was to bring forth the following two understandings:

First, our behaviour/actions are a direct result of what have we been fed with. This is an ongoing process that is delivered to us by society, as a whole. This includes our family, friends, and all of those individuals with whom we come in contact, even on an infrequent basis / daily basis. Our action is the result of whatever we have learned, and our reaction to their actions is the outcome of the skills that we have been able to pick from that long list of teachings that are sewn into us. We can now clearly say that we all are programmed by the society.

Second, how to greet the people we meet, is a small task that has been intricately explained in the above examples. You can see here that our behaviours/styles/words/actions, all change with various age groups that we come in contact with. There is a kind of set-of-instructions that we follow in each case.

I conclude this chapter and leave a gist of the take-away from it; The society inculcates within us, numerous attributes that build up the sets of instructions that we use on a daily basis.

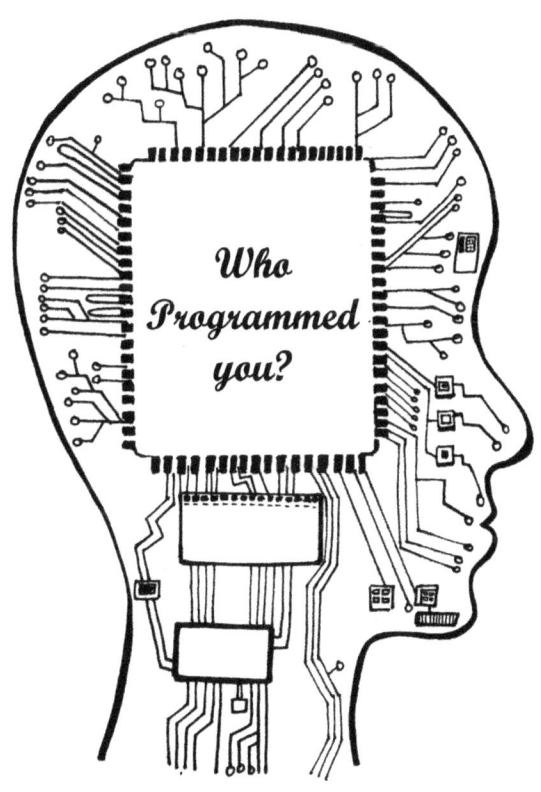

CHAPTER - 2

Understand your daily life programs

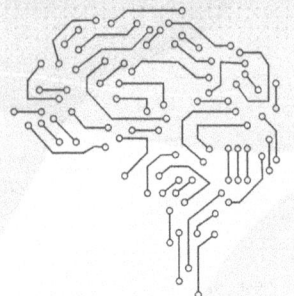

The Similarities between the human mind and computers are more numerous than the differences. One of the key similarities is they follow a set of instructions.

I'm sure you all must have returned with your mugs of coffee, or tea. I am personally a tea lover like most Indians. And I take my own sweet time to make the finest cup of tea for myself. My wife sure makes that good 'karak chai', but I prefer my version!

In the last chapter we see that our mind performs a set-of-instructions to perform any activity.

So, let us discuss how do you make your splendid cup of tea. Here's what I want each of you to think about. Just try to identify in your mind the steps that you take to make tea. Many would say that keep the pan on fire and put in all the ingredients, and there you are! A perfect cup of tea. But don't you think that that is an ambiguous form of interpretation?

Now we all know how to make 'chai', but we ought to define the steps clearly and crisply.

Understand your daily life programs

Steps required to make a cup of tea:

1) Take a pan
2) Take half cup of water & half cup of milk and put it in the pan
3) Now put the pan on the stove and turn the flame on
4) Add 1 spoon of tea-leaves and 1 spoon (as per your taste) of sugar in the pan
5) Let it come to a boil
6) Put the flame on sim
7) Occasionally, switch the flame from high to low. Repeat this, maybe five times. OR Switch the flame to sim when the boiling tea comes up, then increase when it goes down. Repeat this five times.
8) Strain the concoction through a sieve. Your hot cup of tea is ready to sip, enjoy!

Understand your daily life programs

 You must be wondering why I brought up this example. My main intention of doing so was to bring clarity that any activity you perform you follow a set-of-instructions, and it is not easy (not so difficult too) to breakdown your actions into smaller unambiguous tasks. In order to achieve this, you would need clear thoughts in your mind.

Let us take a few more examples and try to get a deeper understanding of the 'set of instructions' that we follow in order to complete any given activity.

Example#1

Ever wondered what protocol should be chosen to cross a busy road?!

We all know that before crossing a road, we need to look left and right, but even this seemingly simple task, the flowchart gets into the action, and each of us exhibits

Understand your daily life programs

something indifferent, or is it somewhat similar? The steps that we take or the action that we perform is unique in their own way. There are a few pointers that get activated that aid us in taking the next step. And remember that they first act upon in our brains, and then the action occurs. Considering that you are on foot, here is where I would like you all to focus your attention on the aforementioned:

- **Distance of the vehicle**
- **Speed of the vehicle**
- **Your estimated speed**
- **Width of the road**

The first two, i.e, the distance of the vehicle, and its speed will determine the total amount of time the vehicle will take to reach you. While the next two points, your estimated speed and the width of the road will assist you in the time frame for you to safely cross the road. Now if the time taken by the vehicle is more than the time taken by you to cross it, your brain would give you a green signal that this is the best time to cross.

In my opinion, there are a few more parameters that we need to look at while crossing the road

- **The lane in which the vehicle is approaching** also makes the difference. If the vehicle is coming in the first lane, even if it is at a lesser distance, or a wee bit high on speed, we will still decide to cross the road because we have to cross the first lane only till the vehicle gets closer to us.

Understand your daily life programs

- **The size of the vehicle** will determine our next move before crossing the road. A different perception will be at play if we were to see a truck and in case there was a motorbike, our flowcharts would actually act differently. Because of the awareness that a two-wheeler occupies minimal space than a truck! In fact, even psychology suggests that in our minds we introspectively will let a truck or a big vehicle pass us by, even if there was enough time and space to cross.

At this point, you must be feeling that there can possibly be no other parameters that we assess before crossing the road. But my dear friends, there is much more. The reason why I am dispecting this situation in such tiny detail is that I want you to understand the intricacies that a human brain explores, in order to successfully attain a given challenge, even if it were to cross a road!! Actually, there is more

- **Weather** or climatic conditions will also draw a different plan in our minds. If there was heavy rainfall automatically, we will switch to the safe mode before taking our first step. Since the roads become slippery, or there could be waterlogging as well, so the whole flowchart changes its course.

- **Road conditions** will lead to conflict in the mind. A bumpy, potholed, or just a rough road would force our minds to engage in a more methodical pattern of moving ahead. Forget about running on such a road, your speed will considerably slow down because your reflexes will be at par with the action plan that would be generating in your head.

Understand your daily life programs

- **Day/Night** time also provides a slight variation in the action that will be executed. For obvious reasons in the daytime, we have perfect vision and clarity of what is around us. Though in the night hours that becomes a challenge.

- **The weight on our shoulders** will automatically alter our speed.

And last but not the least, on a lighter note, we do take a peep as to whether it's a male, female, or a youngster at the driver's seat! Yes, you too do the same, don't you?

- **The age of the driver** plays an important aspect because our reaction depends a lot on who is at the driver's seat. A youngster would be far more impatient and quicker on the nerves, while an aged person would not mind slowing down or even applying the brakes just for you. And if it's a lady driver, we are positive that she will let us pass!

Example#2

What is the first thing you do when you wake up in the morning!?

Understand your daily life programs

Many of us may be early risers, but an alarm is something, that we invariably set before hitting the bed.

I know that there may be many who do not snooze, or some don't even need to set up alarms. But without a doubt, I'm sure that everyone will enjoy reading this portion mentioned below.

Our entire day's output essentially revolves around the time we get out of our beds after a good night's sleep.

So, what is the first thing one normally does once the alarm goes off?

The flowchart that is at work is going to vary in some cases yet most of the time, it remains the same. This activity does not pertain to whether you wake up at the right time or if the snooze activity has to start. So, in the given scenario, I ask people to share with me the exact steps that they usually follow. The various answers that I got were somewhat like, 'I go to the washroom first thing, while another said I drink a glass of water,' so on and so forth. But my reply to them was that there is so much that you are skipping. Most of the answers also pertained to facts like, 'I snooze the alarm, or, one said, 'I turn off the alarm!' I know most of you must be wondering what goes on after the alarm goes off, that is of so much importance! Well, that's the beauty of this book.

Understand your daily life programs

Let me take you to the delicate detailing...!

The flowchart that generally follows, has a list of thoughts. Following are some of the common ones:

#1: Did the alarm wake me up, or did I get up on my own?

If it is the alarm that has woken me up

#1.1: is it the first, or second snooze?

>#1.1.1: If it is the first snooze, I happily go back to sleep for the next golden ten minutes!
>
>#1.1.2: If it is the second snooze, you try to keep your eyes open, which normally doesn't happen!
>
>#1.1.3: If by any chance, it is the third snooze, you spontaneously pick up your mobile, or the alarm clock to check the time!

If it is NOT the alarm that has woken me up

>#1.2: The next best thing one does is look for sun's rays. Your head automatically turns towards the window etc that might be spreading the golden pearls.

And if those pearls are seemingly bright

>#1.2.1: You go, O My God, I am late again! You get into a panic mode, and hurriedly grope at your watch, only to realize that you will be late for that Monday meeting, or early breakfast at a close relative's place!

If day light is not there

>#1.2.2: you feel you have woken up early,
>
>#1.2.3: you reach out to your mobile and see the time to ensure it is not the time to wake up

Understand your daily life programs

BUT...IT DOESN'T END HERE!!

After point 1.2.3, before you decide to sleep again, what do you do? Because I know that you pick up your phone quietly, and check your messages? Yes, I got you! You all do.

I mostly pick up this last point when in seminars to lighten up the atmosphere. And there everyone goes, 'o yes, we do!'

DON'T YOU THINK THERE IS AN ABILITY IN ME TO READ YOUR MIND?!

So, this is what the "DECODE YOUR MIND" really is all about. We have a set system in our minds, whether we agree consciously or not, but that is what takes its little steps and advances to the next.

When we were younger, or many of you may still be blessed with your mother's acting as the alarms. They would wake us up at the set time, yet in their hearts, they always knew that the snooze is going to be at least 4 or 5 times! Our mobile phone alarms and alarm clocks do not speak to us, but when it's the mother waking us up, there are sweet messages that fall in our ears, at every snooze. Let us look at this in detail.

• **Snooze#1:** 'Get up my dear, it's time to go to the office/school,' etc(uth jao beta, school janay ka time hogaya hai)

Understand your daily life programs

- **Snooze#2:** 'You will get late my dear'(beta late hojayega)

- **Snooze#3:** A mother's real love,' Will you get up now, or shall I get my shoe!'(uthna hai ya joota lekar aun)

And after the 3rd snooze, none of us want to sleep anymore, unless we are ready to take the shoe!!

This is getting fun now!

Before I move to another fun (next similar example), let me reiterate few things about the concept here

First, I wouldn't agree more if you would say that you do, or do not, follow the exact same steps. But, without a doubt, the pattern will be somewhat similar. So, apparently, there is a flowchart at work in your day-to-day activities.

Second, it is not easy to drill down to a minute level. But it is fun doing it... The more you practice, the easier it will become for you to understand the flowchart.

Example#3

Let me take you to one more light situation where I want you to imagine yourself having woken up at the 3rd snooze, and you do not have any time to waste. What is the first activity you would do? Yes, you would jump out of the bed and rush to the washroom to get ready for the day

Understand your daily life programs

and get moving. And, good lord, someone else is using your bathroom!! (Assuming it can be used by other family members). Now what all do your reactions involve? What all activities do you indulge in? You have to think in absolute detail.

To this, the people in the seminar burst out laughing! What a tricky situation, right? Here you cannot miss your school bus/meeting in the office. On the other hand, your favorite place, the bathroom, has been invaded!

When, in discussion, the common reactions/answers that I usually got were:

I will use the other bathroom

I will go back to bed

...so on and so forth!

I would like to ask everyone here, and I want a fair answer, are you comfortable using someone else's washroom? Wouldn't you want to know how much time he/she would take inside? And isn't it, your first, happy choice to use your own bathroom?

Don't tell me you also had the same answer??!!

In another situation, when the answer came, "I will take a nap,' at this I prompt another question, 'wouldn't you check the time, and see if you were getting late?"

Yeah, I read your mind again! Or maybe not! But just give it a thought, isn't this the pattern that most people follow?

Understand your daily life programs

The next poll went to a bunch of people who reiterated that if they were up before time, they would undoubtedly just pull up their comforters, and take a power nap!

Now I would also like to ask, that, assuming you have the buffer time, doesn't it matter who is there inside the bathroom? Here I add yet another clue, what if it's your younger brother or sister who has occupied the most awaited room early in the morning!

Now that younger sibling has had it! he/she is going to get a piece of your mind! So there starts all possible, not so descent, comments, and all the banging on the door. The profanities get louder and meaner until the door suddenly opens! And wow! It's that ultimate feeling! Right?

NOW FOR SURE, YOU WILL AGREE THAT I CAN READ YOUR MIND!

DID I JUST HEAR, 'YES?'

These steps, which I am referring to, are actually our minds that have been coded, and by using reverse engineering (calling it as Decode), will you be able to understand how the mind will function. I would like to call it, "Decode Your Mind (DYM)".

Let us now get into the practice of understanding how powerful can the concept of "DECODE YOUR MIND" really is.

In order to benefit from any new concept, we need to understand:

1. Firstly, your conscious mind needs to accept that you need to bring this change, and a continuous process will have to be activated, till the time it gets embedded in your subconscious mind.

2. Secondly, it is imperative to drill down all the attributes to the minutest levels possible because unless our subconscious does not absorb it, we will not be able to utilize it.

So, get into the habit of forcing down this amazing concept that has the potential to prove to you, how amazing you can be!

YES, DECODE YOUR MIND, IS THE WAY TO BE!

CHAPTER - 3

Decode / Read the minds

*I have more conversations in
my head than I do in real life*

―――――――― ✦✦✦ ――――――――

In the last two chapters, we got an insight into a program that is contained in our brain that enables us to function and carry out our day-to-day activities. It is, therefore, imperative, to understand the concept as to what that programming is all about. And, my dear friends, that concept is, 'DECODE YOUR MIND.'

Let us start on a light note. It may make you laugh a little bit, but it will surely solve the purpose!

Mother to Son: Can you please get me Red Label from the market.

Son: Half Kg or One Kg?

Father to Son: Can you please get me Red Label from the market.

Son: 375 ml or 750 ml?

It is funny and odd at the same time, right?

Most of us are aware of the fact that Red Label is a famous tea brand in our country, and there is a fine brand of scotch with the same name, too. The son was, apparently, able to quickly relate the hard drink to the father, and tea leaves with the mother.

It is a rather small example but goes on to convey the deeper meaning. We are always able to understand the exact meaning of what is being said/asked. There is always so much more than what words really mean.

Psychology has done a great deal of research and developments to get into the mindset of people. There have been extensive studies that relate to the understanding of the human psyche. If we take a closer look, we will be able to understand that the psyche of an individual depends on what kind of a flowchart he/she is carrying, that could have contributed from their life's experiences too. This flowchart is connected to the people we meet and situations we get into. From the moment we take our first breath, we get connected to this unavoidable flowchart pattern, that makes or breaks our personality.

Now let us take a different side of this 'science'. To fully hear and understand someone, do you think you need to be aware of their sensory actions only or their mental activity? Well, you need both. Reading other person's mind becomes an important factor because if you have high sensory awareness, you can receive and decipher what is going on with others beyond the words they speak. This highlights your creative intelligence which pertains to a subtle yet concrete understanding of the grey matter of others, that is constantly at work.

Let me now tell you the secret to how I was able to understand precisely, what was it that was going on in the

Decode / Read the minds

minds of others. But honestly, it is not really a secret. It was just my ability to look into the pattern that they would have eventually followed. To be able to gauge the next steps of an individual, all one needs to do is decipher their programming before they act/react in accordance to it. As mentioned earlier, and a fact that everyone is aware of is that we are all programmed by society. This is a philosophy that is so much under our skin that at times we don't even realize it. One just needs to be consciously alert, because society is similar for each one of us, therefore, our/others actions are something that we are inherently aware of. The trick is to be quick! This brings us back to the concept of learning how to effectively read the psyche of someone, and in order to be able to do that, we have to first have the foresight to gauge our own, and for that you need to read (DECODE) your own mind.

#Before my next case study, I would like to add that in India, onions are an integral part in our cuisine. It is not just the base of all the recipes, but our salad is considered incomplete unless onions are served. In fact, most of us are more than happy to have a complete meal with a good amount of freshly cut raw onions salad.

Ankit, a very close person(friend/brother), once came over for dinner. This was many years ago. He was young, unmarried, and trying to balance life out in the college hostel. Of course, life was not tough for him, but staying away from family and the comforts that come along with it, can be quite a struggle on its own. So, my wife laid down the dinner table with lip-smacking delicacies and all of Ankit's favorites! We watched him eat every dish to his

Decode / Read the minds

heart's content. He is one of those people who are very close to my heart. As we ate, we talked, laughed, celebrated the meal. As we were doing the rounds of filling our plates with the varied delicious dishes and salad, Ankit abruptly blurted out that, are onions costly this season?! To this, before my wife went about discussing vegetables and the prices in that typical lady-like manner, my brain was instantly at work and began to process the various facts, doubts that must have gone through Ankit's mind and I answered Ankit that "No! radish is cheaper."

My wife questioned, Ankit is talking about onions, not radish, have you heard him clearly. But I was confident about my thought process and was sure that I have connected to his psyche to decode his mind.

The garbling went to various stages, scenarios and the conclusion was not hard to identify. Instantaneously, I had queries pertaining to his comment. The first one said, "despite the fact, we had served him sufficient onions in the salad plate, why is he even asking that vague question? The second-best thought that popped into my grey matter, and the most valid one, was probably he is not being presented with onions at his regular eat out/dhaba (roadside food stall in India), and, bang on, I was correct!! You see, Ankit was in a hostel at the time and apart from the hostel mess, these youngsters would often eat out. And of course, the pockets were an integral affair. So, with the fixed resources the dhaba's would cut down on vegetables and substitute them with cheaper ones. Because radish is cheaper than onions during

Decode / Read the minds

winters, radish is more frequently and abundantly served in a salad, and not the onions. That is where the comment from him, was intricately presented. The touch of humour only helped me in understanding the perception of his current situation.

I am very well aware of the fact that my subconscious is a very active part of my brain and personality. It is constantly drilling down everything that is going on around me. And this does irritate me at times, because this aspect of mine is always 'in action', even when the need is not there! On the contrary, I feel pretty proud of it too!!!

Sharing with you all one such incident, I call it 'the angry-funny' one! Here my mind was at its drill down mode and surely, was not needed, at the time. So, here goes.

My son had to be dropped off to his school bus-stand, and we, father son duo started to walk, and just as we moved, my son saw a crow sitting on the back of a cow.

My son: 'Papa, I feel that the crow and cow are friends.'

Me: I just smile at him with a 'hmm' sound.

After few seconds

Me: Son, I found one reason for this

Son: tell me

Me: There is only one alphabet, 'r', in cow and crow, that is different.

Son: he smiled and we kept walking

Me: Son, I found a very good reason why they are friends

Decode / Read the minds

Son: tell me...

Me: Okay first you tell me what does the crow do all the day

Son: caw caw (he made the sound of a crow)

Me: that's why the crow likes the cow because he keeps repeating the whole day (caw caw caw)

Some of you may put this under the bracket of, PJ, or poor joke. But doesn't it convey the intricacies of the drill down approach that was at work? Indeed, it does! It helps you to, logically, relate both the sides of the interpretation.

In the onion/radish example, you can clearly see that despite the fact that the question was on onions, the answer lay in radish! And how was I able to read Ankit's mind, and also point out the correct answer? Well, it was purely because of the phenomenal concept that tuned me into acquiring this skill, called, 'Decode Your Mind'. Now you will agree that "Decode your mind" not only helps you to read your own mind but helps you in reading the other person's mind too. It is just a question of believing in it and practicing it over.

CHAPTER - 4

What more to Decode (DYM & Psychology)

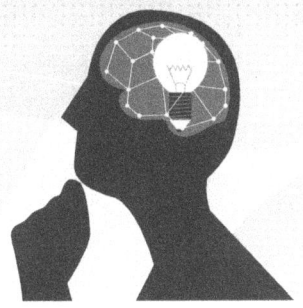

*If you can read my mind,
you'd know how hard I tried*

✦✦✦

Trust your inner voice

So far what we have learned is that our behaviour / actions / reactions are a kind of programming of our brains that is the outcome of the experiences that we go through throughout our lives. And decoding this algorithm is the key to reading the minds of others. In order to get a hold of this practice, and understand the intricacies, you need to start decoding your mind first.

In the following chapter, we will see that this entire talk about the 'mind' is not merely a 'mind game', but it is deeply rooted in human psychology.

In the mode of DECODING YOUR MIND, there is a relevant connection between the head and the heart. Because to get in touch with the flowchart pattern of an individual, you will have to know how the engine is working. By engine, I mean, the heart.

If you can take control of your senses, and others', better known as, sensory perception, you will become a pro in scanning the thoughts of people around you. It is categorically, not an art, but a practice we all need to

What more to Decode (DYM & Psychology)

indulge into.

How important is the coordination between:

- The heart
- The brain
- The gut.

If there is a unified equilibrium in all three mentioned above, you will begin to energetically receive from the world around you. Sensory awareness includes an inward awareness of your reactions, not just in a conversation, but in any given situation. Your retort might be in relevance to what is being told to you, but there is always another element that is at work. And that is the heart's point of view. All of the output that any human being gives/exhibits, is an outcome of a mixture of thoughts and ideas that have the heart at the base of that grinding machine. It is indeed an accomplishment if you can sense people's desires, disappointments, needs, frustrations, hopes, and doubts when they cannot or have trouble articulating these experiences themselves. This also goes on to show that you are a sensitive individual who has the humaneness to feel others, in the literal sense of the word. It takes courage to successfully delve into that part of the human heart, that feels pain. Being sensitive doesn't mean being weak/insipid. It primarily goes on to show the strength of your innate character. Often, we experience melancholy, distress that leads to incomplete/half-hearted tasks because the passion goes missing. The catch here is the 'vibrations', or 'energies. If your energies and vibrations are in your control, you will

What more to Decode (DYM & Psychology)

be able to perceive the same in others. This has got a lot to do with you as a human being.

- How sorted are you
- How happy/sad are you
- Whether you are in touch with your inner self or not

All of these above mentioned are the means of attaining happiness not just in your sphere, but the world, as a whole. The perception/judgment that is created gets into our basic nature at a tender age. When we are very young, all of life's events keep getting registered. And at that impressionable age, some of the understandings of life, people, existence, get engraved for good. That is why we say that the inputs that children are fed within those formative years, should be positive and happy. The conditioning that happens in the early years of our lives will undeniably have an impact on the adults we eventually grow to be. Therefore, if you allow yourself to be sensitive- to feel deeply and empathize with others- you are more capable of making a substantial difference.

My dear readers, you must all be wondering that why am I getting different aspects in 'DECODE YOUR MIND.' They may seem a bit irrelevant, but as you read along you will be able to understand the connection between all of the ensuing aspects. So, rest assured and see the unfolding of minor things into major ones.

In the previous chapters we talked about a philosophy that most of you may believe, and that is, that each one of us behaves differently in a given scenario! While I have a

What more to Decode (DYM & Psychology)

different conviction and theory of the same. I strongly believe that all of us behave in a non-dissimilar (similar) fashion in any situation!

'Parvarish', or upbringing, is one of the most important factors, that determines the quality of the codes that one exhibits in their day-to-day actions. Your family background, that determines your set of values or principles, along with, the experiences that you have been blessed with. All of these attributes provide inputs to the design of your respective flowcharts and determine the entire make-up of your behaviours. Your complete conduct will be the outpour of the extract that the above-mentioned ingredients individually are attributed with.

The parameters that define the flowchart are so huge, that the variations are bound to occur. The more the similarities in two people's upbringing/family backgrounds, etc, the more similarity in their ways of bearing will be seen, and similarly. The more the difference in the nurturing/life's experiences, etc, the magnitude of their being dissimilar widens. The more we are able to understand the similarities, and dissimilarities, the better will we be able to read their minds, and identify their actions.

What more to Decode (DYM & Psychology)

 To conclude what we learnt here that our actions are not just driven by the mind, but the heart and the gut feeling also plays a role here to drive our actions/behaviour. So in order to understand how another person can behave / has behaved, not only you need to decode the mind, you also need to decode the heart of that person. Another point we learnt that two different people provided they have same background they will behave the same way, although the definition of same background is so big that the background of two people will change and hence their behaviours become different.

Recap and what's more

 Before I start sharing how we can use Decode Your Mind (DYM) as a tool to enhance some of the important skills, let us recall / summarize what we have learnt so far

Whatever we do in day-to-day life, it has a kind of set-of-instructions that we follow and it is something programmed by the society based on our experiences.

We are so much into following these instructions, that we never see them at a minute level. The DYM tool has explained how can you visualize these tasks into smaller fragments or in other words zoom out the situation at hand, and check the list of activities we perform in order to attain victory over it. The breakdown into smaller chunks, I call this, 'The drilldown approach'.

It is not easy, neither is it difficult to drilldown your actions into smaller unambiguous tasks. All you would need is a clear and crisp thought pattern. If practiced religiously, this ability to break down any given situation into little parts, would aid you to carefully align the set of instructions in your flowchart. And once this is accomplished, no task will ever turn out anything, except how you wanted it!

Once you have practiced to drill down every thing, you will realize, you upfront can read your behaviour and not just your own mind, you will be able to read other person's mind also. In order to read other person's mind, you have to put yourself in other person's place to see how your flowchart works in that scenario. You might say here that everyone has different flowchart, they are programmed in different environments, then how come reading my mind is going to help here. The answer is, people do not behave so differently in a given scenario. Just try to relate with the examples I used in this book, the detailed level flowchart, I presented in each example, is that too different from the behaviour you/anyone has. If you are able to identify what's there in other person mind upto 70-80% that's a big step towards reading other person mind.

The person behaviour just not a mind game, it is also heart game. In order understand the behaviour we have to see it from logical and emotional angle.

Let me relate two different words I am using interchangeably. When I say Drill Down approach or Decode Your Mind, it is actually looking yours/other' activities in small unambiguous statements. With Code / flowchart / Algorithm, I mean the set-of-instructions a person follows to complete a task. there is a proverb (बाल की खाल निकालना) which means viewing the things minutely. Although it is used in more negative sense for arguing about something which is not important or case when someone is trying to introduce a quibble. But if you relate this proverb, it is almost same what we are doing by DYM-Drill Down approach with a difference that we are doing it purposely.

DYM-Drill down approach is going to help in different areas in personal life, as a leader, as a software developer and in project management. This is something, now we are going to cover in following chapters

CHAPTER - 5

Emotional Intelligence

Emotional Intelligence allows us to respond instead of react

—— ✦✦✦ ——

To be emotionally intelligent means to understand emotions of yours and others and to handle it properly

What has been the buzzword in recent years? Yes, **Emotional Intelligence(EI) or Emotional Quotient(EQ)**

I would like to explore how DYM is tool to improve our EI/EQ. Before we discuss that, I feel lets understand what is EI and also see the importance and value that is attached to us in the light of EQ/EI.

In the following chapter we will just focus on EI and its importance and in the next chapter, some essential interrelatedness will be explored with relation to DYM (DECODE YOUR MIND) as a tool that glorifies EQ/EI.

Let's start with the question here

What is more important in determining life success — **book smart or street smart?**

This question is of a debatable nature, because the contrast between cognitive intelligence (IQ) and

Emotional Intelligence

Emotional Intelligence (EI), runs almost parallelly.

Proponents of so-called "book smarts" might suggest that IQ plays the most critical role in determining how well people fare in life. Those who advocate for the importance of what might be called "street smarts" would instead suggest that EQ is even more important. So, which one is it?

Before proceeding further, let us talk about the 'human need.' What is it that we are working so hard for?

The other day, I was surfing channels on my TV and was hoping to find something interesting. On one of the channels, a Babaji (self-proclaimed Godman) was giving 'pravachan'. His words caught my attention when he said that all the theists out there who bow down in front of God Almighty every single day, feel that they are not expecting anything in return. It is a selfless, devoted act that they perform day in and day out, all they say is God I don't want anything but just keep me happy and bless me with peace of mind, always! *(prabhu main apse kuch nahi mangta, sirf mann ki shanti aur khushi pradaan karo)*

Now, understand this 'selfless wish', "God please keep me happy!". Rings a bell?? Yes, I knew it would!!

You are actually asking the entire world from God! You will be happy only if you have the health, wealth, family, status, position, etc, etc, the list is endless!

Just get into the 'reflecting mode', and think as hard as you possibly can, aren't there only two major levels of 'emotions' per se? Or shall we say 'categories?' I leave that to you. The first emerges to be 'HAPPY', and the

Emotional Intelligence

second, 'NOT HAPPY/UNHAPPY.'

So, apparently, the very first learning that we get from this is that all the hard work, sweat & blood that we are putting into our lives, is just for that one thing, and that is "happiness". It is 'happiness' for ourselves, our families, and our loved ones!

Isn't it so?

Yes, I know that all of you will agree to this! And there is another thing where our thoughts will not differ. And that is, keeping oneself happy is indeed an art. There are people who could be earning just a few thousands and being happy in the real sense of the word, while a millionaire might still be searching for it!

Sharing a quote at this point;

"In today's world, the only person who is happy, is the who knows that no one is happy"

If I see from the perspective of a leader, his/her teammates are not giving their services or putting in efforts, just because of money. The larger reason is that they are doing so in order to be 'happy.' once the leader understands this, his/her topmost priority will become the analyzing of the reasons that build up this 'happy component' of each and every team member. The leader will get persuaded to judge the other person's emotions, and the sole reason would be the outcome in terms of a 'happy individual.'

And a similar mind pattern should get invoked in the members of the team. This will instil in them the ability to not get swayed, or panicked and disheartened at minor setbacks. When we are working in a team, not everything goes as planned. At times it is best to let go and ignore and just forge ahead with a positive mindset.

*Emotio*nal Intelligence

EI first came into existence in the year 1990. Mayer and Salovey have been the first to have coined the term. Later in 1995, Emotional Intelligence won extensive popularity by American psychologist, Daniel Goleman. And his book, "Emotional Intelligence" 1995, won much-deserved acclaim and recognition.

We have leaders who have emotional intelligence are more likely to realize when pride and emotions are influencing their thinking, allowing them to make more rational, impartial choices. In addition to reigning in your own feelings, emotional intelligence makes it easier to anticipate and respond to others' sentiments.

When talking about a leader, we have to understand that in order to build a happy, and consistent, result-oriented team, he/she will have to work on the practice of EI at a very significant level. It may seem tricky, but the sailing will get smooth if the empathy and concern factor remains intact at all times. We have leaders who have emotional intelligence are more likely to realize when pride and emotions are influencing their thinking, allowing them to make more rational, impartial choices. In addition to reigning in your own feelings, emotional intelligence makes it easier to anticipate and respond to others' sentiments.

Emotional Intelligence

EQ is an attribute that masks the big difference between the good performers and the significantly outstanding and great ones. It pertains to the evaluation and final outcome of managing the behaviour, the ability to steer through social complexities, and the choices that one picks that bring about fiercely positive results. End number of studies have been carried out and numerous studies have been exhausted in order to understand EI. But the one psychologist that I would like to speak about here is Daniel Goleman He is an internationally known psychologist who lectures frequently to professional groups, business audiences, and on college campuses.

According to Goleman, there are five key elements of emotional intelligence:

- Self-awareness.
- Self-regulation.
- Motivation.
- Empathy.
- Social skills.

The above-mentioned points are, in some way or the other, related. But let us first take them one by one.

Self-awareness is all about knowing your personal strengths and weaknesses and having a strong sense of your own worth. In order to be able to bring out the strengths of others, we ought to be in absolute awareness of ours first. We all have weaknesses in us, but they can be overcome if we are able to identify them in the first place. We take medicine for an ailment only after we get the diagnosis. No diagnosis or missed diagnosis will only give rise to bigger issues.

Self-regulation too speaks about managing emotions.

Goleman found that self-regulated people **can calm themselves down when they're angry or upset,** and cheer themselves up when they're down. They are also flexible, and adapt their styles to work with their colleagues (no matter who they are), and take charge of situations when necessary.

Whether a leader or a team member, it is imperative for every human being to be able to access their bouts of situational feelings, under tabs. If one is able to do that, more than half the battle is won.

Motivation is that feather you wear in your hat when your drive for life is on an all high. An individual who understands the importance of self-love can forever remain motivated. There should always be scope for self-improvement because that is what will aid you in constant growth in life. Life is a combination of the good and bad. Not everything happens the way we want it to. To be able to forge ahead with rejuvenated spirits is the true mark of a successful human being. Goleman's Motivation states as having an interest in learning and self-improvement. It is having the strength to keep going when there are obstacles in life. It is setting goals and following through with them.

Empathy is the ability to understand and share the feelings of another. In today's world, people have become very practical in life. They always want to find a logical and reasonable understanding of things, situations. They want a scientifically substantiated outlook on practically everything that surrounds them. We are all turning into machines. Simply working, meeting deadlines, and going crazy in this mad world, we forget the biggest yet simplest point, being empathetic!

For how long will we find true happiness in machines and gadgets. At the end of the day, we need someone who genuinely cares for us. And this care turns millionfold if we have the ability to love them back. To be able to understand the feelings of people around you, be it home, workplace, or a whole community. If you are cold enough to never be able to touch their hearts, you have essentially failed in life.

Goleman says Empathy is generally defined as the extent to **which one has the ability to understand and accept another's feelings and emotions.** He adds, empathy—one of the basic components of emotional intelligence—is a critical part of social awareness, and, as such, key to success in life.

Social skills are the emotional intelligence skills to properly manage one's and others' emotions, to connect, interact and work with others. If empathy is outward-driven to the others, social skills are inward-driven and focus on how to interact with and leverage others to reach our goals, Goleman says.

As I had mentioned earlier, Emotional Intelligence encompasses a list of selected traits that are interdependent and interrelated. The absence of even one of them will yield temporary, and weak results. Even if they look positive, they will be short-lived. A mix of all the points enhances the growth of an individual. And it is apparently clear that we can grow, only if we have the ability to bring growth in others.

THE BENEFITS OF EI. Increasingly we are working in organizations with different cultures, genders, generations, geographical locations, work pressures. The following points will benefit you tremendously if you follow EI

- Think before you speak
- Develop meaningful long-lasting relationships
- Understand others
- Enable others to become more productive
- Improve your communication style
- Be proactive with situations that create conflict

To conclude here, this chapter has given an insight into EI and its importance. We saw that to become a great personality, not just IQ, but EQ also plays an integral role. Its actually, even bigger than the IQ!

In the next chapter we will explore, how Decode Your Mind acts as a tool to improve upon our Emotional Intelligence

CHAPTER - 6

DYM- A tool to increase your emotional quotient

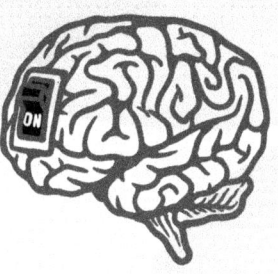

Tact is after all a kind of mind reading
- Sarah Orne Jewett

So far, we have gathered that the concept of DYM enables us to intricately read/understand our own minds and the minds of others too. It is an effective tool that provides leverage into the psyche. The expansiveness of this tool/concept can be witnessed in the way we are able to foresee the actions that we/others exhibit.

Now let us take some examples to demonstrate the importance of EI

#1

We all are individualistic personalities with distinctive traits, and that is what defines our uniqueness. A friend once shared a story of his workplace. He talked about one of the employees who had reacted in a rather absurd manner at one of the regular meetings, and thereafter, the poor fellow had been tagged 'fool'. And it was no other than the boss who had assigned this tag. Now, how do you all feel about this? Some may agree that it is appropriate to address a 'fool' as a 'fool', or an 'idiotic' person, and not as anything else!

DYM- A tool to increase your emotional quotient

In my opinion, the balance between the IQ and EQ was certainly not carefully struck by the boss. By doing so, the boss is probably unintentionally letting the self-esteem of that individual down, and that, according to me is not the trait of a good leader/boss.

#2

An empathic leader goes more into the background of the outcome of any task. Say if any task is not completed then will you treat your team member in the same way every time imply lashing out, pinpointing the fault/error, in other words, reprimanding, will not solve the purpose. You have to find the root cause and drill down skill will help you analyse it out to see:

- Is the action intentional?
- Is there a lethargy or a laid-back approach?
- Is it that the individual has put in a 100% effort, yet the results are not up to the mark?

Now based what was the cause your action will change

There is quote which I follow very strongly

"If you have to choose from what is right and what is kind, always choose what is kind, because that will be always right."

If you relate right and Kind with reference to emotional intelligence, right means logical/rational right and kind means right as per EI, you can see that EI right will always be right.

DYM- A tool to increase your emotional quotient

In many of the movies we heard the similar dialogue, where your thought process ends, my thought starts from there. Same way I can say where IQ (logically right approach) ends, emotionally right things starts from there.

With above few examples / quotes, you can understand the importance of being with strong EQ.

Now let's see how the DYMs Drilldown approach helps us improve on Emotional Intelligence components.

If we relate **self-awareness** (a component of EI), we will find its coexistence in DYM. The ability to understand the behaviour in a more concrete manner, the inherent qualities of DYM enables you to zoom in on your actions that further gives depth and clarity on a logical level to all about knowing your personal strengths and weaknesses and having a strong sense of your own worth.

If you try to search for how we can be more aware of ourself, the pointers you will find will be around following lines:

1) Determine your values

2) Decide your future plans

3) Focus on what is your passion, what you enjoy doing

4) Discover your strengths and weaknesses

You will agree that no one else can know you better than what you know for yourself. So as part of self-awareness, what is needed, you should be able to check your self with a lens, where you can drill down your behaviours, your thoughts, your actions and your words. And when we say

DYM- A tool to increase your emotional quotient

drill down / go in more depth, DYM is the tool which makes you think on micro level. So this tool in practice will able to make you aware of yourself.

Self-regulation too speaks about managing emotions. We have seen that self-regulated people can calm themselves down when they're angry or upset. Once you are aware of what triggers your anger (or any other emotion) you can always control it easily. Once you have decoded your behaviour, it is just making amends or modifying the flowchart. It is art to correct your flowchart to control your emotions.

In one of Bollywood movie (Munna Bhai MBBS), there is a character (Dean of the medical college), he is shown to be very short tempered guy and to control his anger, he has trained his mind that instead of showing anger he will laugh and has convinced himself that instead of shooting up his blood pressure, he can take the benefit of laughter therapy. This is the example of self-regulation where when I say he trained his mind is actually he has done amendments to his flowchart he has to follow when he is angry.

We all are born with typical personality traits. Here I am not talking about the physical features. We all are beautiful, and we know that! But here the discussion is about those inner-personality traits that actually add beauty to your outer personality as well. One of those aspects has a significant role and relevance in determining how impactful your personality really is. Yes, EMPATHY, is what I am talking about. Without a doubt, you would all agree, that Empathy contributes to

DYM- A tool to increase your emotional quotient

the golden attributes in an individual. A very minute detailing goes into understanding what is going on in the other person's mind. And those intricacies can be touched upon with the help of DYM. We learned earlier that this seemingly simple task can be brought to fruition only if you have expertise with DYM. It will enable you to get into the shoes of the individual you are dealing with, at that given point in time. As expressed, various times, each one of us catapults different traits that stand us apart from each other. The ability to perceive the working of the flowchart of an individual gives you an insight into his/her working of the mind. DYM empowers you with attaining clarity of whatever is going to be the next action/reaction of someone. Once you have perfected this craft, you will even be able to rationally recognize the background, or, in other words, the origin of that typical scenario, if you were well versed with DYM. It will aid you in taking the right course of action, and trust me, friends, you will never falter. DYM also equips you to bridge the gaps with empathy. And once you are laden with the empathetic factor of DYM, half the battle is as it is won!

So, we have learned here that DYM helps you in building the 3 components of Emotional Intelligence (EI), namely, Self-Awareness, Self-Regulation, and Empathy. And to take right decision it is equally or more important to view the things with eyes of Emotional Intelligence rather than just being logically right.

CHAPTER - 7

Decode the Situation

Don't judge a person without full understanding of the situation. Just because you don't agree, doesn't mean you're right.

Effective leaders need to be flexible and must adapt themselves according to the situation –
P. Hersey & K. Blanchard

The last two chapters on Emotional Intelligence gave us an in depth understanding of the relevance of EQ (Emotional Quotient) in making a headman/leader. And it is the inclusion of DYM that aids in attaining the various components of EQ/EI.

In this chapter, we will throw light upon, behavioural patterns with relation to the ensuing situation.

Many of you must be blessed with children, and without a doubt, they are the ones that make our lives complete. Undoubtedly it is the most rewarding yet challenging aspect of an individual's life. Parenthood essentially contributes to our personal growth. They are our true reflection. Whatever mode of upbringing we use, they become a mirror image of it. And, that is why, even earlier I have said, that your attitude towards your children should be one of precision. Younger kids need more

Decode the Situation

cautious handling because they are at that impressionable stage of their lives, that a small act, or, even a look/glare, the volume of your voice, will make or break that personality. In households where the parents have a rather rough demeaner often find their children out of their control. Yes, at times, the situation does demand us to make our point understood to the child, and it should be rendered at the right time with the right strategy. It may get difficult at times between the choices at hand, and your mental framework as compared to your heart, **which may pick the 'polite' parent type, rather than the aggressive one.**

*2

Another scenario also speaks on similar lines. But the game role is totally different. Yes, I am talking about the role of a leader/headman and whether the decision taken by them, with relation to a team, should be **logically right or emotionally correct.** Because here you are dealing with people who, in the broader aspect, define your success. The knack that a boss must be equipped with, has got a lot to do with their grip on the arms and ammunition that would be required to tackle a situation.

Now, let us take a dive and look deeper into the above-mentioned scenarios. When I ask the audience which approach (soft/hard one) should a person go for, the answer that I normally get is that there should be a balanced approach. And if I define and elaborate on the word, 'balanced', it does not at all mean a wavering of the thought process. There has to be a stable mindset. As a

Decode the Situation

parent, you cannot flip from a strict parent to a happy-go-lucky kind. Just because you had to be stern and uncompromising, you should not get overly lenient, too! Actually, here balance revolves around the demand of the situation. Based on the situation only, must you define which way to go.

My aim is to extend far down and make you gauge the situation aptly. In other words, I am trying to enhance your drill-down abilities. And this is what I exactly mean when I say 'Decode the Situation'

First, we will explore by taking the parent-child relationship example.

If we see from the parent-child perspective, it is beyond any doubt that we as parents have seen a lot more of life than what kids could ever fathom. Then, many a time, 'unwanted pieces of advice', are an outcome of the life's experiences that we have matured in. We genuinely care for our children and do not want them to suffer at any cost. We understand that kids are still like clay, and any bit of wrong/misinterpreted thoughts may leave their personalities permanently disfigured. And that is why all the suggestions, counselling, etc, are always 'on'.

I am sharing the following lines which I read on social media but it is very heart touching and defines the gap between parent & kid relationship.

Do we care or, Do we control ???

I was in conversation with a middle-aged couple. They

Decode the Situation

started fighting right in front of me. The upset husband said- See doc....I 'care' so much for her & this is what I get in return... To which the fuming wife replied- He doesn't care...he just 'controls'...!

The care from one person was perceived as control, by the other! Made me wonder, **what is care, and what is control?? How to identify them??**

Soon I got the answer.

I had an argument with my teenaged daughter over a trivial disciplinary issue. Harsh words were exchanged leaving both of us in tears...

After some time, as our emotions settled own, we said sorry to each other. My daughter hugged me and said- Papa, you know why you got upset? You were not upset because I did wrong, but you were upset because I didn't follow your instructions.

There is a big difference...!

I was stunned by her mature thinking pattern. I received my answer too. I was trying to control her under the disguise of care and that caused the conflict. If I really 'care' for someone, I will not get upset or angry with that person, I will keep searching for different ways to help him/her out. If I am struggling in any relationship, I need to closely observe if there is any subtle control, hidden behind my apparent care, because:

- Care is an expression of love; while control is an expression of ego.
- Control cuts; Care connects.

Decode the Situation

- Control hurts: Care heals.

Keep caring for people but do not control them because often people are not wrong, they are just 'different'...

Keep caring...

I believe the above story explains what I mean by 'the balance'. This is an eye-opener for me to manage things based on the situation.

If you are a youngster then please do not use this tool as a means of emotional blackmail to your parents. Because if I present the same view from a different perspective, you will understand what exactly I am trying to convey.

In a parent-child relationship, things do tend to get a bit complicated at times. Say, for example, there are 10 cases where a parent/parents gave some form of guidance to their child/children. Now out of these 10, 6, or 7 could be actual care, while the rest could be 'control'. We will not get into that graph here. What I am trying to stress, is that the child/children feel that the 6 or 7 points in question are control, and the meagre 3 or 4 is care. Dear children, I want to let you know that all of that is the outcome of absolute care and nothing else. All you kids out there have to understand this and learn to 'balance the situation', in order to see the care, come across.

Now let us see it from the leader's perspective:

Before we move ahead, let me discuss the different leadership styles and the concept of 'Situation Based

Decode the Situation

Leadership.', and also assess which of these is a better leadership tool.

There are basically 6 different leadership styles, we are going to cover in this topic

- **Coercive** Leaders demand immediate compliance
- **Authoritative** leaders mobilize people toward a vision.
- **Affiliative** Leaders create emotional bonds and harmony
- **Democratic** Leaders build consensus through participation
- **Pacesetting** leaders expect excellence and self-direction
- **Coaching** leaders develop people for future

The question arises which leadership style is better?

Many people feel that the style any leader opts for would be a reflection of his/her own basic traits. But that is not true. But the ability to choose a technique depending upon the situation is what makes the best headman. The style matching with the leader's trait will be easy for him/her to implement but they will need to practice other styles as well, to easily adopt it when the situation demands.

Situation leadership concept helps us to define the situation.

Decode the Situation

There are 4 main stages of SL (Situation Based Leadership)

1) Stage 1: Telling, Directing, or Guiding

2) Stage 2: Selling, Coaching, or Explaining

3) Stage 3 – Participating, Facilitating, or Collaborating

4) Stage 4 – Delegating, Empowering, or Monitoring

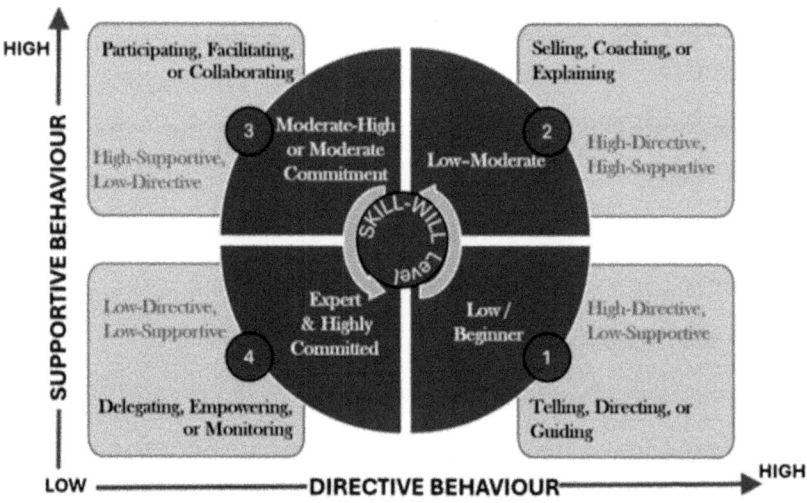

So how does this work?

If your team is in stage 1, you are acting as pacesetting leader, in Stage 2, you will act as coaching leader. In stage 3, you act as a democratic /affiliative leader whereas in stage 4, you will act as an authoritative leader.

None of the leadership styles are neither above nor below one other. We cannot say for a fact that the 1st or 2nd etc is a better choice. The leader must decide in accordance to the maturity level of his/her team members, and only

Decode the Situation

then can there be assured success.

So, the answer to the question, which is the best leadership style, stands at, 'it depends'.

It's a challenge to filter out what is the best tactic when it comes to dealing with so many brains out there. Whether it should be all practical and reasonable, or whether it should beat around the emotions attached? Here is where the role of the action seeker will come in. By action seekers we normally get an image of someone who is all-powerful and invincible. Before winning a literal battle, the everyday battles have to be won.

The above explanation (parents-kid relationship and leadership styles) shows that what style you need to adopt does not depend on your basic trait, it depends on Situation.

Let us now try to understand the connection with DYM: First, its drill down approach aids us to understand the different aspects of the situation in a better way. So, basically if one is able to acquire the understanding of the situation of someone, the expertise to recognize their actions gets sorted.

Second, it will help you also to switch your mind from one style to the other that befits the given situation. We will be able to regulate our mannerisms and traits in accordance with the demand, and not just harp around our basic characteristics.

Decode the Situation

I will now share a couple of more examples that will reveal that they have the same soul, but appear to be at a 180-degrees contrast.

#1: Customer is God VS. Customer is not doing any favor to us, they pay for the services.

#2 Whether you should be aggressive or patient:

You will agree that in the above lines a parallel approach will have to be adopted that is directly in relation to the given situation. Whereas if you opt for any 1 out of the 2, you are sure to fail at some point or the other.

Let me now take my own example and explain further.

I have been blessed to have worked for some excellent organizations where my credentials were duly acknowledged. I took up roles that were very demanding, and the fighter that I have always been, I emerged victorious wherever I went. At one point in time, I was in a leadership role as the HR head of a very well-known, esteemed establishment. The strength of the team under me was roughly 10 people, and the total number of employees was about 600.

All you HR professionals out there, can truly identify with my situation, right?

Human resourcing is one of the most challenging roles that one could possibly ever get to understand. It needs the ability to differentiate between the character of an

Decode the Situation

individual, with his/her skill sets. It is one of the tasks of HR professionals. After spending a number of years in the IT sector, the HR role was not only new but seemed very exciting too. It was a challenge that I just had to take up, and prove to myself that I could do this too!

My duties not only included hiring new staff but also maintaining cordial relations with the entire team. And this is a big team that we are talking about!

I was put in different slots by different people. By slots I mean, some graded me as a genuine, sympathetic manager, while others categorized me as rude, harsh, and too very blunt for their comfort. Now question here is why they have so much different opinion for me. I did have to play the bad guy for the sake of the situational demand. I was not being 'bad', literally, but I had to set boundaries and adhere to strict actions with certain employees. That deemed me as an unsympathetic, stonehearted monster who simply doesn't care. But, you see, that was not so. The reason why I switched between roles, as that was the need of the hour. The 'SITUATION' was such that I had to wear different armours at different scenarios in order to justify my role. There was a contrasting conflict that went into the minds of different people with regard to my true personality.

But the above-mentioned situation cannot tag me into being multifaced / arrogant, or compassionate / considerate. It is absolutely natural for people to label me,

Decode the Situation

and I do not have a problem with that. They will be able to decipher my actions if they were in my shoes. Honestly, there were times when I amused my own self by switching from my character with relevance to the situation. And I would really think to myself, was this really me, or is it the dual side, that is the real me??!!

Living with two different opinion / traits, you might relate it with a dual face personality, But I will not call it a dual-faced personality but will say it is my glorified trait and I should be proud of the fact that I am able to change my trait based on the situation to accomplish the task/goal assigned to me.

I am not a dual-faced personality because I do not have the habit of beating behind the bush, and also my role does not compliment that. I always gave out clear messages verbally and where I had to restrict my words, my body language spoke volumes. My focus always remained on the integrity of the company and the different tools that were presented to me when I took up this role.

 I would here summarise the take-away from this chapter, you need to decode the situation and act/react accordingly.

CHAPTER - 8

Decode the Intention / Feeling

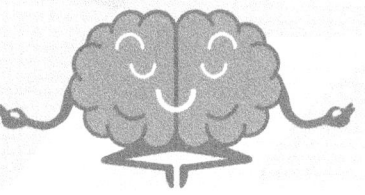

Maturity is when someone understand their situation and don't hurt them back

———— ✦◆✦ ————

In the last chapter we uncovered the hidden traits that come into play with the shift in situation. Which primarily means that we must scan the attitude of an individual with respect to the situation that he/she is in, and then club it all together to make sense out of it. And not get judgemental, because that is your weakness, and this has got nothing to do with the one you are dealing with. In order to identify with the actions of any one, a drilldown will come into play, and this drill down is connected to the intention of the person.

Another attribute that now emerges, is the 'INTENTION'. There is always a deep link between the thoughts that conspire to the actions, so it is evident that we must first get into the thought-mode of someone before reaching to a conclusion. In simpler words, understand the intention/feeling, rather than just the actions/words.

In the end of the last chapter, I took my example and share how come I switch between different traits and people judges me with what kind of treatment I gave

Decode the Intention / Feeling

them. Some of them call me rude and many of them call me a friendly leader. So lets discuss how come we can identify the actual trait of person with two or more traits he has shown many times. So answer is try to understand the intention of the anyone's action, which I am calling as decoding the intention.

I would like to tell you about a gentleman who held a prestigious position in the same organization where I was the HR head. He had the personality, the charm, the intellect, and the experience, and I truly admired him. He pulled off his job profile with ease, and calm, but because of the position he too gathered some hatred down the line. There were both youngsters and older team members with reference to age, and life's experiences. While some misjudged him and even quit their job, others understood him for what he truly was. Quoting an incident that revolves around a very young employee who disagreed with the attitude of this gentleman, let's call him Mr. X. He mistook Mr. X's arrogance as rude, demanding, and inappropriate. Whilst, another employee who was older, and definitely more sorted, understood that if Mr. X did not behave the way he did, everyone around him would take him for granted. The youngster could not relate to the fact, that it was the situation that prompted Mr. X to act in a certain way.

Apparently, Mr. X was a very empathetic leader but because of his 'SITUATION', he too tasted the wrath and hatred of a few, just like how I experienced. We both connected well as we were pretty much on the same boat.

Decode the Intention / Feeling

Often, we do go wrong in giving judgment. If a boss speaks loudly, his tone is often misjudged as arrogance. But the reality is that the harshness/bluntness of his/her tone could be the result of the position they hold. Their authoritativeness is because they have the experience behind them which involves the required expertise. To be able to point out an aspect in a situation, which may not even strike the rest of the team, is a trait that a true leader possesses, or should possess. The pattern/way of the flowchart of such individuals aids them in bringing out the best of themselves, and their teams. They unwittingly do the rounds of pinpointing, and yet get the desired result. One has got to be very certain of their abilities because the connection between the intellectual brain and emotional brain can go for a toss at any given point. It can be the result of an argumentative, audacious team member, or an overconfident extrovert. Because bosses have a very special task at hand at all times. They are not only answerable to the topmost management but are responsible for the growth and brand of the particular organization/company. It becomes their baby and no lag is neither expected nor accepted, which would in any way, hinder the progress of the place they work for. The team members do misinterpret the attitude of their bosses and may feel let down or even insulted, but the fact remains that there is a lot on their shoulders.

Friends are our chosen family and there are times when we feel closer, and more connected, and at ease with them than even the blood relations themselves. But we all do experience highs and lows, don't we?

Decode the Intention / Feeling

Now imagine you meet a very good friend of yours, and a little action from him/her, upset, and even hurt you. And you do begin to think in your mind, 'this is not fair, or, is this person even bothered about me!! Yes, we all go through such phases. but later, the event/incident/context unfolds before you and you instantly get it! The intention of that particular friend was not meant to harm/hurt/upset you in any which way. You are able to correlate from where your buddy is coming from, and you almost instantaneously switch from the earlier feelings of disappointment/despair. And begin to feel all right. Your perspective takes an opposite turn!

More on decoding the intention, let's dig deeper. There is an intention behind every action the same way as we have feelings behind our words. So, we ought to decode the feelings, and not jump to conclusions by staying stuck up on the literal meaning.

#1 Housewife/Homemaker

In general, they are used interchangeably for those wives who are not working professionals. But if we dig deep and zoom out these phrases with a lens (DYM tool), you will find 180 degrees difference between them.

A deeper insight will bring more clarity. What is the thing that comes to your mind when you hear the phrase, 'housewife'?

A wife who is not earning money does not go to the office and sits at home etc. Does it not give you a feeling that she is like a liability, whereas, if you see the word homemaker

Decode the Intention / Feeling

in-depth, you will get the feeling that she is the one who takes care of the house, and herself, now this word (homemaker) gives you the feeling that she is an asset to the family. Assets and liability are the opposite of each other. So, you can see these 2 non-dissimilar are so much similar.

Let me take another example where 2 phrases that seem to be similar are so dissimilar.

#2 'I live with my mother' VS. 'My mother lives with me.'

How do you interpret the above-mentioned lines? For many, it will be the same thing that Mom & I live together. But like the last example, if you think in detail, they are opposite in the manner that when I say Mom lives with me, she seems like a liability, where I am representing myself as the head of the family. Whereas, when I say, I live with my mom, it gives a feeling that conveys that mom is the head of the family and she has greater importance in the family.

So, you see, how feelings play an important connecting factor in this scenario.

Your choice of words plays a crucial role in making the intention/feeling understood.

When working in a team, where you are the leader, it is possible that people make mistakes. And you being the headman, becomes your responsibility to point it out to whosoever committed the error. Your intent behind it would not be to let that person down, but it was important

Decode the Intention / Feeling

to point it out. Now let us say that that worker/team member responded in an instant, 'if you felt bad then I'm 'sorry'. So, what do you think, was that person genuinely sorry or was it just a spur of the moment 'comment', and says, 'I am sorry'! Now let us scan this line with 2 conflicting aspects.

First: Do you feel that the person has accepted the mistake and that is why rendered the apology? You may feel so, but I would disagree. I would say that the individual is apologetic because you, the leader/boss has felt bad about the action committed, but he/she is oblivious of the mistake per se, in simpler words, he/she has not understood the mistake that has been committed. The second aspect would be more appropriate and comforting in the way that, the team member does not feel that he/she has been at fault, yet is empathetic enough to have said sorry.

There is politics involved in every workspace throughout the world, and there is no denying that. Be it a small setup, or a vast organisation, the degree may vary, but this one never goes amiss! Similarly, in the corporate sector, the level is nourished by many such phrases! For instance, I HAVE VS I COULD HAVE VS I MUST HAVE. Now there is a difference that cannot be ignored. I HAVE, indicates, that the person is certain about whatever is in question/context, while I MUST HAVE, conveys an indefinite feeling with respect to the outcome of an action/situation. And I COULD HAVE coneys a more befitting possibility that the individual may take liability of the action.

Decode the Intention / Feeling

Our body is an excellent source of conveying what is going on inside our heads. Yes, our body language (physiology and tonality) is the greatest weapon that we put to use when words are either not required, or are not enough to express the true feeling. This diagnostic helps us attain:

- A clear understanding of what the second person wants to convey. And, if need be, correct them, too.
- Your choice of words can assist you in being the better leader. If you are in tune with your inner most feelings, then it is undeniable that you will ever pick incorrect words.

Yes, we all want to be the best managers, but in order to do that we need to start thinking a bit differently. Because the challenge is not to become a manager, but a leader. I would now take up some extremely relevant set of phrases which may seem similar, but on taking a closer look you will get the scent of the intention that is being touched upon and you will find the second phrase has much more depth.

First set of phrases are:

1. Delegates responsibilities

2. Delegates authorities

In the first case, it is clear that the manager is giving you a job for which you are totally responsible. The outcome of that assignment, for instance, and whether it is going to be good or bad, will solely be connected to you. While on the other hand, the leader is delegating you with the authority of carrying out the same task. This actually

Decode the Intention / Feeling

means that you are not just responsible for the outcome of the task but you have the power to make decisions, and in such a case scenario, the end will invariably turn out to be the most appropriate one.

Now the next set:

1. Drives team members

2. Coaches team members

In both cases, the task has to be brought to fruition. In the first case, you will feel a kind of push without any motivation whereas, in the second case, you will get more guidance, hand holding from your leader which makes you feel that you are on the same boat as your leader. This will not only increase your subject knowledge but also keep you motivated.

And the next set:

1. Seeks control

2. Seeks commitment

If the team is told that the boss is seeking to control which is going to be the dominating aspect here. If we go with the commitment, there is absolute coordination and integrity that will be witnessed.

Someone who 'seeks' commitment, is undoubtedly, the better leader. There is a personal attentiveness that is witnessed, and it is of a far important value that is being fed into you. It becomes a sincere obligation, and the response to it is beyond all goodness.

Last but not the least:

Decode the Intention / Feeling

1. Presumes

2. Explores

While working on a project/assignment a lot goes into ensuring successful completion of the same. In order to understand the outcome, a manager may be judgemental without going in-depth whereas a good leader will connect with team members, will listen to them without any biases/beliefs so that he/she explores the background of what good/bad outcome has emerged, and this helps them make the right decision. When you are exploring, in the real sense of the word, you are essentially identifying to the situation, not the person.

CHAPTER - 9

EQ & IQ relationship

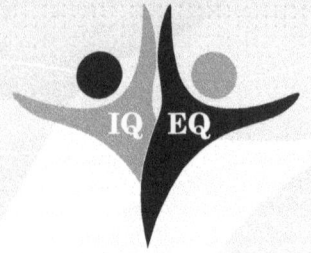

IQ wins the race and EQ wins the life.

———— ✦✦✦ ————

IQ gets you hired and EQ gets you promoted

This chapter is more on understanding how a high IQ (Intelligence Quotient) person can attain a high EQ level (Emotional Quotient) as well.

To understand this, we need to go into a debate on what these quotients are and how they are related. It is only after the analysis will be able to understand whether it is possible to achieve both or not.

The general saying is that a person with a high IQ cannot have an equally high EQ, because of the fact, that the left brain is responsible for IQ while the right brain takes care of the EQ!!

I will refer to HUMAN INTELLIGENCE as the topmost level of all intelligence components whether it is IQ / EQ or any other, if at all another exists!!

We already have discussed a lot on EQ in this book and IQ is not alien to any of us. We have been taught about IQ right from junior school up to our major academic learning years. But we surely get the essence of it after we go through this biggest learning, called 'life.'!

EQ & IQ relationship

Comparison between IQ & EQ

1. IQ tests assess your capacity to think critically, solve problems, and comprehend and communicate complex ideas. EQ exams assess your ability to perceive and respond to emotion in yourself and others, as well as your ability to use that awareness to make decisions. EQ can be used to predict how a person would react in a given situation.

2. IQ is a number that represents a person's relative intellect; it is the ratio of the mental age as recorded on a standardized test to the chronological age multiplied by 100. The ability to acquire or grasp new situations; how to reason through a particular problem/scenario; and the ability to apply knowledge to one's current surroundings are all factors that are measured by IQ. The neocortex, or top region of the brain, is most affected.

Whereas, Empathy, intuition, creativity, adaptability, resilience, stress management, leadership, integrity, authenticity, intrapersonal skills, and interpersonal skills are all traits of emotional intelligence.

3. Many studies have found that EI is a greater predictor of success than IQ. There are numerous explanations for this. However, emotional intelligence is a stronger predictor since it demonstrates how much a person can control and adjust his or her actions in everyday life. IQ tests do not assess this.

EQ assesses how you interact with others. To lead or start a successful firm, you must be able to hire and manage competent and efficient employees. To achieve

EQ & IQ relationship

this effectively, you must persuade individuals to work together in harmony, which necessitates managing numerous people's emotions. In comparison to a person with a low EQ, a person with a high emotional intelligence may effectively manage this. This is something that an IQ test cannot determine. Also, persons who are good at managing other people's emotions have better social and romantic connections. High-IQ people are more likely to be antisocial or socially dysfunctional. People who have a high level of emotional intelligence are more socially and societally accepted.

A very interesting point has come to light, and I would love to share it with all of you. A lot of people have a preconceived notion, that a person having a tech background cannot be a good leader! Because according to them, such an individual would have a higher IQ level as compared to a non-tech person. And their EQ (Emotional Quotient) levels would not be at par so as to put them in that bracket of the high EQ group.

EQ & IQ relationship

But I completely disagree on this one. Pardon me if I sound audacious here, but I too am a tech background holder, and I am all for EQ as an equally important attribute.

My success story took me from a programmer par excellence to delivery head, and eventually landed me human resourcing. I, never in my wildest dreams, ever imagined that my career would span such contrasting profiles. But the fact remains, that I excelled in each and every role that I ever took up. So, if I was originally a techie, who was expected to behave like one, how come I did justice to a position like human resourcing? The answer is inevitably clear. I was able to strike a balance between my IQ & EQ because I always understood their unpreventable co-existence. My day-to-day actions were an amalgamation of consciously focussed mental and emotional thoughts.

Once I was discussing with one of the senior persons of the same reputed organization where I was heading the HR profile, on my journey from software programmer to HR Head. I told him confidently that I am good in HR because I was an excellent programmer. He chuckled and smiled back at me and asked, how are these roles related? And then I explained him the concept of DYM – Drill down approach.

We have extensively discussed on the DYM- Drilldown approach and how through it, we attain the ability to break the units in the smallest parts possible, which further enriches us to understand things in great detail.

EQ & IQ relationship

We also learnt that with the help of DYM you can read, not just your mind with more precision, but the mind of others too, which further ordains you with great EQ levels. In other words, if you master the breakdown skill, you can achieve unmatchable EQ.

An individual with a high IQ level is directly linked to problem solving. And we are also aware of the fact that there are pre-defined steps that we must go through, in order to get the desired result, or solve a problem. High IQ people are naturally equipped with the different flowcharts that are imperative in different situations. They quickly adjust their flowcharts as and when needed. If there arises a problem, these people instantaneously switch to the most apt flowchart.

Isn't the IQ concept similar to DYM-Drilldown approach? Did I hear 'yes'?

Yes, these are akin to each other.

In the next chapter, we will dwell into the concept, that

A high IQ individual is undeniably, a good programmer because he/she is well aware of the coding that goes along the way. When we create a program, we have to follow the steps wherein the desired algorithm is put into place after extensive drilldown. After writing these steps, which the computer also understands, you will be able to put together the best codes that will bring about the perfect programming. This also means that that a high IQ person is already adept to the concept of drilldown, and has pretty much, mastered the skill.

EQ & IQ relationship

I remember mentioning about myself earlier on in the book, I would like all of you to also know, that in my younger days I was totally fascinated with mathematics, and programming. I would spend many hours on these two, and would always have the longing to know more. My career graph also has many years of teaching the two subjects, but of course, that was at the beginning. The concepts related to the two subjects intrigued me to the core, and so much so, that I started to develop my DYM-Drilldown understanding in every aspect of life. And, believe me, it worked!

Now, when I try to analyse that how/why was I able to make my people management/leadership role, a grand success, was because of the fact that I was good at reading the minds of people. And I understood that if you hurt/disregard someone, they will never support you. While managing people in the company, under the role of HR Head, I obviously never struck upon any one's feelings. Not because I wanted to look like the best guy around, but because I genuinely cared for each and every team member. If I clearly would assess that xyz person has a soft point that will create ripples in his/her persona, why would I ever prick it! There were many instances that gave me an understanding that by deeply reading the minds of people, so many characteristics evolved inside of me. The drilldown approach/mind reading practices helped me build the empathy factor, and many other components of EI. Even at a time I was only subconsciously aware of this thing called, 'empathy', I still excelled in my leadership role, and that was primarily

EQ & IQ relationship

because of the fact that I was able to zoom into any aspect. Whether it was my own mind, the minds of people, or a programming statement.

 So, in the light of the above I would like to say that a high IQ person is already unconsciously/unknowingly aware of the Drilldown approach. So, the only major task at hand is to add the same set of skills with respect to basic psychology of the human brain. In order to decode the mind by including this very aspect, the coaching will involve the psyche that will witness the birth of something extra ordinary. And, dear friends, this was the main reason behind my statement that I always made for myself, I am unbeatable at EI concepts only because of the fact that I have a high IQ level.

CHAPTER - 10

DYM – Base to the Programming skills

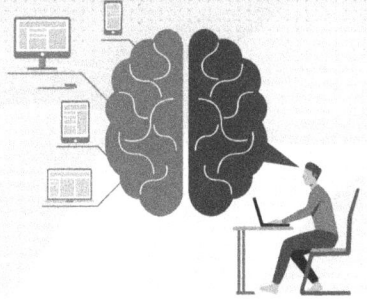

Programming is 10% writing the code and 90% is understanding what to write.

❖❖❖

Any fool can write code that a computer can understand. Good programmers write code that humans can understand.- Martin Fowler

So far, we have learned that DYM is a great tool that increases your EQ and invariably, helps in people management. Let me now share how this tool helps you in becoming a great programmer. Not just this, in the next chapter, I will share how DYM helps you in project management too.

Before I share how it is useful in programming, let me share you few things about my background so that you can relate things in a better way.

1989 was the year when computer education had recently taken a boost. And around the same time, I too got inclined to computer programming. I still remember that flowcharts were added as a mandatory part in the mathematics syllabus. My dear friends, it was at that time when I clearly understood two things that got registered in my mind for good. And those two things were the start of my DYM journey that got materialised

DYM – Base to the Programming skills

after almost 3 decades. Those two golden points were;

• Computer is a dumb machine: it cannot do anything on its own.

• Any real-life activity that we perform is a programming statement.

A little bit more to my background, I gave good 16 dedicated years to IT and software development. It was only in 2013 that I decided to move into the education sector, and then for the next 5 years I started giving coding lessons, where in I also taught programming fundamentals and data structure using C++ language.

So, whenever I would start a new batch, without any conscious effort, the first two hours would revolve around teaching the concept of decode your mind. A good teacher invariably shares thoughts/lessons that will aid in equipping his/her students. And I instantly always got rewarded, and that came through the eyes of my students who could completely identify with DYM. They clearly understood that it would prove to be the finest tool to build their programming abilities as well.

Programming was not a new term for my students. They had a very basic knowledge and understanding of the same. So, my very first question that I always threw at them was that, in layman language, please explain what is programming according to you. We would create a fun scenario where I would tell them to explain about the concept of programming to me, considering I was their parent who had zero knowledge about it.

DYM – Base to the Programming skills

So, they go on to say, computer is a dumb machine and apparently it cannot do anything on its own. The next question that would pop up would be, how does the computer function at all if it is a dumb machine? And then my students would answer in a similar layman language. They expressed, an individual, whom we call a developer, has done some feeding in the machine, which we call 'instructions. And the computer in return acts in accordance to these instructions, and delivers a certain output. That output is called 'programming'!

Also, these set of instructions must be concrete, with no ambiguity at all. They go on to say, computers follow something called GIGO. GARBAGE IN GARBAGE OUT. In simpler words, if you feed garbage to the computer as instructions, it will only produce garbage. But technologically, if you feed it with incorrect statements, it will create baffling output!

Many a time, students came up to me and said, I have written the perfect code, but it is not working! And to this I would give them a cheeky smile and say, please recheck the code that you have made. Because, without a doubt, you have messed up somewhere or missed out something, else the system would have responded accurately.

DYM – Base to the Programming skills

 Let us now bounce back to DYM. Apparently, programming is aiding the computer with the minutest of details to be able to deliver the desired output, and here is where I ask people, that are you certain of the method / steps / inputs that go on to give exact results from a dumb machine, and if the answer is yes, then it is proof enough that they understand my thought behind the question. Which says that if you have the ability to drilldown every aspect in order to emerge with a fool proof code, your problems are no longer going to be problems. For a machine to deliver your thought process, it is evident that you have pondered on each and every possible aspect. And this is how DYM furnishes you with the ability of being a programmer par excellence.

So, the golden rule stands as, concentrate on the smallest steps, refine them, and then move toward the intricate ones. In simplest words, join the dots and create your masterpiece. Without a doubt, all these baby steps will carve out the highest potential in a programmer. Here I would like to add, a QA individual will find themselves adequately equipped to build their test cases. Because test cases are the outcome of concrete, minute level detailing.

CHAPTER - 11

DYM – Base to the Project Management skills

Failing to plan is planning to fail

――――――― ✦✦✦ ―――――――

Let us now take a peep into how DYM can help you in project management.

Project Managers play the lead role in planning, executing, monitoring, controlling, and closing projects. They're expected to deliver a project on time, within the budget, while keeping everyone in the know-how and happy too!

One of the essential pillars of strength and support that holds up the entire project is the team of highly productive people who entirely devote themselves to it and make an all-out effort to get the job done. In this book, we already learned a lot about people management so we know DTM will help you to strengthen this aspect too.

Another pillar towards project management is the planning component. If you plan well, you will deliver the whole project on time withing the budget. During planning you need to create a workable scheme that will include clearly defined activities, cost estimates, schedule development, and resource planning.

Let us go step by step and assess what is it that a project

DYM – Base to the Programming skills

manager does in the planning phase. The key task in planning is to create the WBS (WORK BREAKDOWN STRUCTURE). WBS is a whole process that aids in conquering large projects to get things done faster, and more efficiently.

Once you have small chunks you can identify the interdependency of the task, estimated time and resources required to complete the task. The whole planning and then the execution of the project depends on WBS. Even if you see the budget, execution, and Monitoring & Control, it is only possible to do because you have the right structure before you.

You know that costing, resource planning and its monitoring, all are easy if we have smaller tasks at hand. WBS is like getting a magnified picture of the whole project. When you have zoomed in; you can track it / control it more minutely. So, all your project management phase is depended highly on your WBS which you build during planning phase.

Now let me share the connectivity between DYM and the process in question.

WBS is the augmented insight of the breakdown of tasks into their minutest frame possible. Similarly, DYM makes you able enough to perform a given activity that comes forth in our daily lives. The difference between DYM and WBS is more literal because of the fact

DYM – Base to the Programming skills

that DYM can be split into tiniest fragments possible, while in the case of WBS, the project would carry on for days, months, or even years to show its final outcome. The task breakdown in both the cases, or the only difference between WBS and DYM is with relation to the time. As with DYM we identify, process, and act. This may be instantaneous or within the framework of a stipulated time. Whereas, WBS is created with deliberate caution because it could be on a very huge scale. And like mentioned earlier, the processing of all the attributes that are to be carefully kept under supervision while painting a project, the time taken in the first stages can also be time-consuming. And once everything is sorted and the action-plan takes flight, another unstipulated amount of time will be witnessed. Of course, those who have worked on the project will know the time frame or scale of the completion.

I am sure that you now understand that DYM is that tool which not only helps you in managing the varied brains that you come in contact with in your work team, but this also assists in building all possible areas that are required to carry out a project. In short, self-management, people management, skills management, IQ EQ management, sorted. All thanks TO DYM.

Take Away

 I would not share too much in summarizing the book, because I'm sure that each one of you has your own set of take-aways!

Decode Your Mind (DYM) is a very simple tool that helps you in reading your own mind, the minds of others, and gives an insight into one of the most powerful attributes, namely, EI/EQ. The glory of understanding EQ/EI is that it equips you with skills that further assist you in becoming better, personally, and professionally. It embarks upon a journey that shows you progressed leadership abilities, and interpersonal relationship skills. Not only this, it also brushes up your programming, and project management prowess.

DYM is an extraordinary tool that shapes your perception, and highlights your personality.

My heartfelt thank you to each and every reader who took out time to read the book.

The sequel of DYM will be out soon. It will help you in attaining your peace of mind, and achieving far-reaching goals.

Your suggestions/feedbacks are always welcome.

I am just an email away: dym@allaboutleading.com

For more contact details, refer the back side of the book.

www.ingramcontent.com/pod-product-compliance
Lightning Source LLC
LaVergne TN
LVHW061558070526
838199LV00077B/7098